D0579516

Diplodocus/Diplodocus

By Joanne Mattern
Illustrations by Jeffrey Mangiat

Reading Consultant: Susan Nations, M.Ed.,
author/literacy coach/consultant in literacy development
Science Consultant: Darla Zelenitsky, Ph.D.,
Assistant Professor of Dinosaur Paleontology at the University of Calgary, Canada

WEEKLY READER®
PUBLISHING

Please visit our web site at www.garethstevens.com.
For a free color catalog describing our list of high-quality books,
call 1-800-542-2595 (USA) or 1-800-387-3178 (Canada).
Our fax: 1-877-542-2596

Library of Congress Cataloging-in-Publication Data

Mattern, Joanne, 1963–
   [Diplodocus. Spanish & English]
   Diplodocus / by Joanne Mattern ; illustrations by Jeffrey Mangiat / Diplodocus / por Joanne Mattern ;
ilustraciones de Jeffrey Mangiat.
     p. cm. — (Let's read about dinosaurs / Conozcamos a los dinosaurios.) Text in English and Spanish.
   Includes bibliographical references and index.
   ISBN-10: 0-8368-9424-3   ISBN-13: 978-0-8368-9424-0 (lib. bdg.)
   ISBN-10: 0-8368-9428-6   ISBN-13: 978-0-8368-9428-8 (softcover)
   1. Diplodocus—Juvenile literature. I. Mangiat, Jeff, ill. II. Title.
  QE862.S3M3322318   2009
  567.913—dc22   2008040418

This edition first published in 2009 by
Weekly Reader® Books
An Imprint of Gareth Stevens Publishing
1 Reader's Digest Road
Pleasantville, NY 10570-7000 USA

Copyright © 2009 by Gareth Stevens, Inc.

Executive Managing Editor: Lisa M. Herrington
Creative Director: Lisa Donovan
Senior Editor: Barbara Bakowski
Art Director: Ken Crossland
Publisher: Keith Garton
Translation: Tatiana Acosta and Guillermo Gutiérrez

Printed in the United States of America

1 2 3 4 5 6 7 8 9 10 09 08

Table of Contents

- - - - - - - - - - - -

Contenido

Boldface words appear in the glossary./
Las palabras en **negrita** aparecen en el glosario.

One Long Lizard!

Diplodocus (dih-PLOD-uh-kuss) was one of the longest animals that ever lived. It was longer than two city buses!

- - - - - - - - - - - - - - - -

¡Un lagarto muy largo!

El diplodocus fue uno de los animales más largos que haya existido. ¡Era más largo que dos autobuses urbanos!

This dinosaur had a long neck that helped it reach food. A long tail helped it balance.

- - - - - - - - - - - - - - -

Este dinosaurio usaba su largo cuello para alcanzar la comida. Su larga cola lo ayudaba a mantener el equilibrio.

neck/
cuello

tail/
cola

7

Diplodocus had big legs but could not run fast. It may have used its tail to fight off **predators**.

- - - - - - - - - - - - - -

El diplodocus tenía patas grandes, pero no podía correr deprisa. Es posible que usara la cola para protegerse de los **depredadores**.

9

Finding Food

This **herbivore** (HER-buh-vor) ate only plants. Its favorite food was probably pine trees. The huge dinosaur ate a lot of plants each day.

- - - - - - - - - - - - - - -

En busca de comida

Este animal era **herbívoro**, sólo comía plantas. Es probable que su alimento preferido fueran los pinos. Este enorme dinosaurio comía muchas plantas cada día.

Diplodocus was too big to walk into a thick forest. Instead, it stuck its long neck between the trees.

- - - - - - - - - - - - - - -

El diplodocus era demasiado grande para caminar por un bosque denso. En lugar de eso, metía su largo cuello entre los árboles.

Diplodocus had big teeth shaped like pegs. Its teeth were good for pulling leaves off trees.

- - - - - - - - - - - - - -

El diplodocus tenía dientes grandes con forma de clavija, buenos para arrancar las hojas de los árboles.

15

Herds and Hatching

Diplodocus traveled in a group called a **herd**. These dinosaurs lived 150 million years ago.

- - - - - - - - - - - - - - -

Manadas y huevos

Los diplodocus se desplazaban en grupos llamados **manadas**. Estos dinosaurios vivieron hace 150 millones de años.

herd/
manada

Diplodocus was a kind of dinosaur called a **sauropod** (SAWR-uh-pahd). Scientists think many sauropods laid eggs in nests.

- - - - - - - - - - - - - - -

El diplodocus era un tipo de dinosaurio llamado **saurópodo**. Los científicos piensan que muchos saurópodos ponían huevos en nidos.

Scientists have found its **fossils** in western North America. They study the fossils to learn more about Diplodocus.

– – – – – – – – – – – – – – –

Los científicos han encontrado **fósiles** de diplodocus en el oeste de América del Norte, y están estudiándolos para conocer mejor a este dinosaurio.

Wyoming/
Wyoming

Utah/
Utah

Colorado/
Colorado

UNITED STATES/
ESTADOS UNIDOS

New Mexico/
Nuevo México

North/
Norte

West/
Oeste

East/
Este

South/
Sur

KEY/CLAVE

= Diplodocus lived here/Zonas
donde vivían diplodocus

Glossary/Glosario

fossils: bones or remains of animals and plants that lived long ago

herbivore: an animal that eats plants

herd: a large group of animals

predators: animals that hunt and eat other animals

sauropod: a large, plant-eating dinosaur with a small head and a long neck and tail

- - - - - - - - - - - - - - - - - - -

depredadores: animales que cazan y devoran a otros animales

fósiles: huesos o restos de animales y plantas que vivieron hace mucho tiempo

herbívoro: animal que se alimenta de plantas

manada: grupo grande de animales

saurópodo: dinosaurio de gran tamaño, que se alimentaba de plantas; tenía la cabeza pequeña y un cuello y una cola largos

For More Information/Más información

Books/Libros

Descubriendo dinosaurios con un cazador de fósiles/Discovering Dinosaurs With a Fossil Hunter. I Like Science! Bilingual (series). Judith Williams (Enslow Publishers, 2008)

Diplodocus/Diplodocus. Pebble Plus Bilingual (series). Janet Riehecky (Capstone Press, 2007)

Web Sites/Páginas web

Dinosaurs for Kids: Diplodocus/Dinosaurios para niños: Diplodocus
www.kidsdinos.com/dinosaurs-for-children.php?dinosaur=Diplodocus
This site has fun facts, illustrations, a map, and a time line./Esta página presenta datos entretenidos, ilustraciones, un mapa y una línea cronológica.

Zoom Dinosaurs: Diplodocus/Enfoque en los dinosaurios: Diplodocus
www.enchantedlearning.com/subjects/dinosaurs/dinos/Diplodocus
Find facts, pictures, maps, and printouts of Diplodocus./Encuentren datos, ilustraciones, mapas e información para imprimir sobre los diplodocus.

Publisher's note to educators and parents: Our editors have carefully reviewed these web sites to ensure that they are suitable for children. Many web sites change frequently, however, and we cannot guarantee that a site's future contents will continue to meet our high standards of quality and educational value. Be advised that children should be closely supervised whenever they access the Internet.

- - - - - - - - - - - - - -

Nota de la editorial a los padres y educadores: Nuestros editores han revisado con cuidado las páginas web para asegurarse de que son apropiadas para niños. Sin embargo, muchas páginas web cambian con frecuencia, y no podemos garantizar que sus contenidos futuros sigan conservando nuestros elevados estándares de calidad y de interés educativo. Tengan en cuenta que los niños deben ser supervisados atentamente siempre que accedan a Internet.

Index/Índice

About the Author

Joanne Mattern has written more than 250 books for children. She has written about weird animals, sports, world cities, dinosaurs, and many other subjects. Joanne also works in her local library. She lives in New York state with her husband, four children, and assorted pets.

Información sobre la autora

Joanne Mattern ha escrito más de 250 libros para niños. Ha escrito textos sobre animales extraños, deportes, ciudades del mundo, dinosaurios y muchos otros temas. Además, Joanne trabaja en la biblioteca de su comunidad. Vive en el estado de Nueva York con su esposo, sus cuatro hijos y varias mascotas.